Barbara Cartland

PICTURE ROMANCES

Barbara Cartland
PICTURE ROMANCES

Illustrated by Gray Morrow and adapted by Charlotte Weaver

M

Macmillan London

ISBN 0 333 33541 4

First published 1981 in the United States of America

First published in Great Britain in 1982 by
MACMILLAN LONDON LIMITED
London and Basingstoke
Associated companies in Auckland, Dallas, Delhi,
Dublin, Hong Kong, Johannesburg, Lagos, Manzini,
Melbourne, Nairobi, New York, Singapore, Tokyo,
Washington and Zaria

Printed in Great Britain by
The Pitman Press Ltd, Bath

Contents

Foreword

When I dictate my novels and do 6,000 to 9,000 words in two and a half hours I see it all happening in front of my eyes.

Gray Morrow has captured very cleverly my heroines – soft, gentle, innocent and pure, but also intelligent and resourceful. They are each every man's ideal woman.

The heroes are handsome, brave, cynical and blasé until they fall in love, spiritually as well as physically, with the heroine. Then she recreates in them all the civility and ideals they had lost in the raffish, sophisticated world in which they shine as sportsmen and lovers.

My novels are written to bring those who read them beauty and love. I hope these cartoons will do the same.

15

THE SIGHT OF STAVERTON HOUSE--THE EARL'S RESIDENCE IN LONDON--LEAVES PETRINA BREATHLESS...

DO YOU LIVE HERE ALL ALONE?

WHY DO YOU ASK?

I CAN SCARCELY IMAGINE LIVING IN SUCH...SUCH SPLENDOR! I SHOULD FIND IT QUITE OVERWHELMING!

I AM GLAD SOMETHING ABOUT ME IMPRESSED YOU!

12-3 © 1980 United Feature Syndicate, Inc.

HER GRACE THE DUCHESS OF KINGSTON ARRIVED THIS AFTERNOON, M'LORD!

AH, WHAT COULD BE MORE OPPORTUNE... MY GRANDMOTHER IS HERE!

MOMENTS LATER...

SO YOU HAVE SOMETHING TO TELL ME, DURWIN... DO I GATHER YOU ARE ENGAGED TO BE MARRIED?

NOT TO ONE OF THOSE ARDENT WIDOWS WHO'VE BEEN BESIEGING YOU, I HOPE!

NO, INDEED, GRANDMAMA! I HAVE NO WISH TO BE SHACKLED TO ANY WOMAN!

THE PROBLEM FACING ME IS QUITE VEXING ENOUGH WITHOUT ADDING OTHER FEMALES!

12-4 © 1980 United Feature Syndicate, Inc.

16

18

12-9

TELL ME, CLAIRE-- WHAT DO YOU KNOW ABOUT MY GUARDIAN AND LADY ISOLDA?

SHE WAS WIDOWED IN THE WAR --AND HAS BEEN A REIGNING BEAUTY EVER SINCE!

THE EARL HAS BEEN HER BEAU FOR MONTHS-- THE BETTING IS, HE WILL BE *TRAPPED* INTO MARRYING HER!

I MUST SAY-- THAT SEEMS A RATHER DEPRESSING WAY TO GET MARRIED!

© 1980 United Feature Syndicate, Inc.

AS PETRINA AND THE DUCHESS RETURN FROM THE GARDEN PARTY--

HIS LORDSHIP WOULD LIKE A WORD WITH YOU IN THE STUDY, MISS!

I AM FLATTERED YOU WISH TO SEE ME-- WHEN SO MUCH OF YOUR TIME IS TAKEN UP BY YOUR LADY-LOVES!

THAT IS NO WAY TO SPEAK TO YOUR GUARDIAN!

20 © 1980 United Feature Syndicate, Inc.

I MEANT NOTHING IMPROPER! I WAS MAINLY REFERRING TO THE LADY ISOLDA... ARE YOU GOING TO MARRY HER?

YOU WERE NOT CALLED HERE TO DISCUSS MY PRIVATE LIFE, PETRINA!...KINDLY SIT DOWN!

12-13

WHAT I HAVE TO SAY CONCERNS LORD ROWLOCK... I GATHER HE HAS BEEN PAYING YOU A GOOD DEAL OF ATTENTION!

ROWLOCK OBVIOUSLY THOUGHT PETRINA WAS TOO NAIVE TO SEE THROUGH HIM... HE IS NOTHING BUT A CONTEMPTIBLE CUR!

HE IS ALSO WITTY AND GOOD-LOOKING...

BE CAREFUL, DURWIN, THAT YOU DO NOT DRIVE HER INTO HIS ARMS!

I WILL SEE HIM *DEAD* BEFORE HE MARRIES PETRINA!

WELL, WELL, WELL!... WHAT AN UNUSUAL DISPLAY OF EMOTION!

Petrina calls on her school friend, Claire, only to find...

MY DEAR! WHAT IS THIS? YOU'VE BEEN CRYING!

OH, PETRINA! I HAD EXPECTED TO TELL YOU THE HAPPY NEWS OF MY ENGAGEMENT-- TO FREDDIE BRODDINGTON! ... BUT NOW I C-CAN NEVER M-MARRY HIM!

WHY EVER NOT? HE LOVES YOU DEEPLY! AND HE IS RICH AND WELL-BORN! WHAT IS THERE TO PREVENT IT?

THE FACT THAT I WAS A FOOL-- AND NOW I AM BEING *BLACKMAILED!*

BLACKMAILED! ...BY WHOM?

SIR MORTIMER SNELDON! ...WH-WHEN I FIRST CAME TO LONDON, HE FLATTERED ME... I--I THOUGHT I LOVED HIM!

© 1980 United Feature Syndicate, Inc.

SO I WROTE HIM SOME S-STUPID LETTERS...

AND NOW HE SAYS HE WILL SHOW THEM TO MY FIANCE --UNLESS--

--I PAY HIM FIVE THOUSAND POUNDS!

OH, PETRINA! WHAT AM I TO DO? WILL YOU LEND ME THE MONEY?

OF COURSE, CLAIRE DEAR! BUT BEFORE YOU HAND IT OVER SO TAMELY-- LET ME THINK WHAT CAN BE DONE!

DEAREST PETRINA! HOW CAN I THANK YOU?

BY NEVER TELLING YOUR FIANCE HOW STUPID YOU'VE BEEN -- TO GET YOURSELF BLACK-MAILED BY SNELDON!

IT IS *SHAMEFUL* TO THINK THAT ANY MAN CAN GET AWAY WITH BEHAVING SO ABOMINABLY!

PERHAPS THERE MAY BE **ANOTHER** SOLUTION!

© 1980 United Feature Syndicate, Inc.

That night at Staverton house, a boyish figure slips out of the library window...

THANK GOODNESS ~ NO ONE IN SIGHT!

To foil Claire's blackmailer, Petrina boldly undertakes to steal back her friend's compromising letters!

BETTER TAKE THE WHOLE STRONGBOX AND OPEN IT LATER! NOW-- IF I CAN JUST GET AWAY UNSEEN!

At that moment, the Earl of Staverton is leaving Lady Isolda Herbert's house...

HOW CAN YOU TREAT ME SO COLDLY, DURWIN? YOU KNOW I LOVE YOU!

I DOUBT IT... TO BE HONEST, ISOLDA, I DOUBT IF YOU HAVE EVER LOVED ANYONE BUT YOURSELF!

© 1980 United Feature Syndicate, Inc.

On his way home from Lady Isolda Herbert's--the Earl is startled by a falling object!

WHAT TH--?!

A THIEF!... HE MUST HAVE DROPPED HIS LOOT OUT THE WINDOW!

CAUGHT YOU IN THE ACT! AND NOW YOU'LL PAY FOR YOUR CRIME, MY MAN!

© 1980 United Feature Syndicate, Inc.

24

12/23

26

Petrina has saved Claire from blackmail -- but her furtive reading of the more outspoken newspapers have made her aware of greater injustices!

SUCH MISERY AMONG THE POOR!...IF ONLY I COULD GET THE EARL TO HELP ME DO SOMETHING!

...BUT I SUPPOSE HE IS TOO TAKEN UP WITH LADY ISOLDA! OH, DEAR! WHAT IF HE *MARRIES* HER?

Next day...

A DEBUTANTE NEEDS GOWNS AND FURBELOWS!...DOES THAT NOT EXPLAIN SUCH EXPENSES?

NO, MY LORD...I PAY HER DRESSMAKER AND MILLINER...MISS LYNDON WITHDREW THOSE SUMS IN *CASH!*

YOU THERE! STAY AWAY FROM THE YOUNG LADY!

NO! IT IS ALL RIGHT!

HERE--TAKE THIS!

OH, THANK YOU, MISS!

Later--after arriving at her friend Claire's house ~~

M-M-MY LETTERS! ...YOU BOUGHT THEM BACK?!

NO--I STOLE THEM, IF YOU MUST KNOW!

...YOU WERE NOT THE ONLY ONE SIR MORTIMER WAS BLACKMAILING! BUT NOW THE EARL WILL DEAL WITH HIM!

27

HOW CAN I EVER THANK YOU, PETRINA?!

BY SWEARING YOU WILL NEVER TELL ANYONE ABOUT THOSE LETTERS--OR HOW I OBTAINED THEM!

OH YES, I SWEAR IT! ...AND WE MUST CELEBRATE!

I SHALL GET FREDDIE AND MY BROTHER TO TAKE US TO VAUXHALL GARDENS-- TO HEAR THAT FRENCH SINGER THE EARL FANCIES!

© 1980 United Feature Syndicate, Inc.

As Petrina returns to Staverton house--

IS ANYTHING WRONG?

HIS LORDSHIP DID NOT SAY, MISS--ONLY THAT HE WISHED TO SEE YOU AT ONCE!

YOU PROMISED THERE WOULD BE NO MORE INDISCRETIONS--BUT I SEE NOW THAT YOU ARE NOT TO BE TRUSTED!

WH-WHAT DO YOU MEAN? I HAVE DONE NOTHING WRONG!

© 1981 United Feature Syndicate, Inc.

IN THAT CASE, WHY HAVE YOU BEEN WITHDRAWING SUCH LARGE SUMS? ...ARE YOU, TOO, BEING BLACKMAILED?

NO--OF COURSE NOT! THERE IS NOTHING FOR ME TO BE BLACKMAILED ABOUT!

THEN PERHAPS I MAY HEAR THE TRUTH...

I-I THOUGHT YOU WOULD NOT APPROVE ...I HAVE B-BEEN GIVING MONEY TO POOR WOMEN IN PICCADILLY!

28

REFORM TAKES TIME, PETRINA ...I HAVE ALREADY SPOKEN OUT IN THE HOUSE OF LORDS ABOUT THESE POOR WOMEN

--BUT YOU MUST NOT BECOME TOO INVOLVED! IT WILL BREAK YOUR HEART--AND MAKE YOU A FANATIC!

THE VICAR OF ST. JAMES'S DOES MUCH TO HELP THE POOR...PROMISE ME YOU WILL SEEK HIS ADVICE IN THESE MATTERS!

KNOCK! KNOCK!

© 1981 United Feature Syndicate, Inc.

YES--WHAT IS IT?

A MESSAGE FOR MISS LYNDON!

OH YES--FROM CLAIRE! I AM TO DINE WITH HER ONE EVENING!

Petrina has been invited to dine at the home of Claire's parents--the Marquess and Marchioness of Morecombe.

YOU YOUNG PEOPLE ARE OFF TO A BALL TONIGHT, I'M TOLD...

ER--QUITE SO, PAPA!

OH DEAR! WOULD THEY NOT APPROVE IF THEY KNEW WE WERE ACTUALLY GOING TO VAUXHALL GARDENS?

MY DEAR, THE PRINCE REGENT HIMSELF GOES THERE! WHO WOULD DARE DISAPPROVE?

© 1981 United Feature Syndicate, Inc.

29

Petrina feels a strange pang as she hears the Earl's other lady love-- French singer Yvonne Vouvray-- perform at Vauxhall Gardens!

HOW CAN HE HELP BUT FIND HER ALLURING?

B-BUT OH DEAR! IF THAT MAKES ME SO *JEALOUS*, I--I MUST BE IN *LOVE* WITH HIM MYSELF!

In the next supper box, she suddenly hears Lord Rowlock and the Duke of Ranelagh---

YOU ARE A BRAVER MAN THAN I, RANELAGH--TO DALLY WITH STAVERTON'S SONGBIRD!

As Petrina listens to French singer Yvonne Vouvray-- other voices reach her---

BEWARE, RANELAGH!

STAVERTON IS A DEAD SHOT! IF HE FINDS YOU POACHING ON HIS PRESERVE --HE MAY CALL YOU OUT!

NO DANGER, ROWLOCK! THE LOVELY YVONNE WILL CERTAINLY NOT INFORM HIM!

SO SHE IS *DECEIVING* HIM WITH THE DUKE OF RANELAGH!...OH THEY ARE BOTH SO ODIOUS!

HOW CAN SHE *BEAR* ANOTHER MAN'S TOUCH WHEN SHE IS LUCKY ENOUGH TO BE LOVED BY MY GUARDIAN?

YOU AND I MUST DINE OUT TONIGHT, PETRINA! MY GRANDSON IS GIVING A DINNER PARTY!

IS IT TRUE THE PRINCE REGENT IS COMING?

QUITE! THEY ARE TO DISCUSS THE GOLD CUP RACE AT ASCOT--WHERE DURWIN'S HORSE WILL RUN AGAINST THE PRINCE'S!

I SEE ...

THE PRINCE LIKES OLDER, MORE SOPHISTICATED WOMEN, MY DEAR! HIS OWN LADY FRIEND WILL BE HERE, OF COURSE ...AND I'VE NO DOUBT THE LADY ISOLDA WILL ALSO CONTRIVE TO GET HERSELF INVITED!

The Earl's dinner party is still going on when Petrina and the Duchess return to Staverton house...

WE WILL JUST SLIP UPSTAIRS WITHOUT BEING SEEN!

THERE IS A BOOK I WANT TO READ IN THE BLUE DRAWING ROOM, MA'AM ...LET ME GO FETCH IT!

Later...as Petrina slips out to the garden before retiring...

IF ONLY I WAS AS WORLDLY AND ATTRACTIVE AS LADY ISOLDA, PERHAPS HE MIGHT--

WAIT! WHO IS THAT--?!

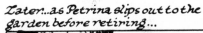

31

PLEASE! DO NOT BE ALARMED!... MY NAME IS NICHOLAS THORNTON ... I AM A NEWSPAPER REPORTER!

HOW DARE YOU INTRUDE LIKE THIS?!

THE EARL IS GIVING A PRIVATE PARTY, YOU HAVE NO RIGHT TO SPY ON WHAT IS HAPPENING AT STAVERTON!

I ASSURE YOU, MISS LYNDON--I AM NOT HERE BECAUSE HE IS ENTERTAINING THE PRINCE REGENT...

I HAVE COME TO REPORT HOW HE ENTERTAINS *SOMEONE ELSE!*

© 1981 United Feature Syndicate, Inc.

REPORTER OR NOT, YOU ARE TRESPASSING! BY RIGHTS, I SHOULD CALL FOR HELP AND HAVE YOU THROWN OUT!

I REALIZE THAT! BUT I ALSO KNOW HOW *KIND-HEARTED* YOU ARE ... SO I BEG YOU NOT TO GIVE ME AWAY!

HOW CAN YOU POSSIBLY KNOW ANY SUCH THING?

BECAUSE I HAVE HEARD ABOUT THE MONEY YOU GIVE POOR WOMEN ON THE STREETS ... WHICH IS WORTH A STORY IN ITSELF!

© 1981 United Feature Syndicate, Inc.

33

"I'VE WAITED MORE THAN AN HOUR TO HEAR WHATEVER YOU HAVE TO TELL ME, ISOLDA!"

"ONLY THAT I LOVE YOU MADLY, DURWIN! MUST I GO--?!"

"OF COURSE YOU MUST!--WITH MY GRANDMOTHER AND WARD UNDER THIS SAME ROOF! AND YOU KNOW HOW SERVANTS TALK!"

"YOU ARE REALLY BECOMING QUITE TIRESOMELY STRAITLACED!"

"IF YOU FIND ME SO TIRESOME-- PERHAPS WE HAD BEST STOP SEEING EACH OTHER!"

"AS YOU WISH, DARLING! BUT I FEEL QUITE SURE YOU WILL SOON HAVE A *CHANGE OF HEART!*"

Without telling the Duchess-- Petrina contrives to be dropped off in Paradise Row--near Mlle Vouvray's house!

"MISS LYNDON...?"

"OH, THERE YOU ARE, MR. THORNTON! HAVE YOU MADE ALL THE ARRANGEMENTS?"

"YES INDEED, MISS! BUT WHAT MAKES YOU SO SURE SHE WILL BE ENTERTAINING THE DUKE OF RANELAGH?"

"BECAUSE MY GUARDIAN, THE EARL, HAS GONE TO ASCOT! AND AS YOU KNOW, WHEN THE CAT'S AWAY--"

"AH, QUITE SO! A PLAYFUL NIGHT FOR THE MICE, EH?"

34.

As Petrina and the reporter wait on the doorstep of an empty house---

THE DUKE'S CARRIAGE HAS ARRIVED!

Later---

YOU, BILL--CALL THE FIRE BRIGADE! SAM--DROP THIS STRAW DOWN THE BASEMENT RAILING OF MA'M'ZELLE VOUVRAY'S HOUSE!

THEN I'LL TOUCH OFF THE *FIREWORKS!*

And presently---

THERE WILL BE EVEN *MORE* FIREWORKS --WHEN THEY LEARN A NEWSPAPER REPORTER IS ON HAND!

LOOK! HERE THEY COME NOW! MADEMOISELLE VOUVRAY AND THE DUKE!

SPLENDID! BY TOMORROW MORNING THEY WILL BE THE TALK OF LONDON!

--AND LA VOUVRAY WILL HAVE NO FURTHER CLAIM ON YOUR GUARDIAN'S AFFECTIONS!

WH-WHAT DO YOU MEAN CALLING ME 'YOUR GRACE'?!

IS THAT NOT THE PROPER WAY TO ADDRESS A DUKE?... I CERTAINLY WANT MY NEWS STORY TO BE ACCURATE!

London is agog with the spicy news that fire drove the Duke of Ranelagh from Mlle. Vouvray's house at night!

BLAST YOUR GOOD INTENTIONS!

BY SHOWING UP VOUVRAY FOR THE BAGGAGE SHE IS --YOU HAVE EXPOSED ME TO PUBLIC RIDICULE!...LEAVE MY PRESENCE AT ONCE!

Later that morning...

I ONLY WANTED TO SAVE HIM!... HAD I NOT ARRANGED THAT NEWS STORY, HE WOULD HAVE BEEN TRAPPED INTO MARRYING LADY ISOLDA!

© 1981 United Feature Syndicate, Inc.

LAWRENCE + MORROW 1-19

OH--GOOD MORNING, LORD ROWLOCK!

I HOPE I AM NOW FORGIVEN FOR WHATEVER CRIME I MAY HAVE COMMITTED!

BELIEVE ME, PETRINA, I WOULD HAVE FALLEN IN LOVE WITH YOU IF YOU HADN'T A PENNY!

DON'T YOU REALIZE HOW LOVELY YOU ARE?...LOSING YOU HAS MADE ME THE MOST MISERABLE MAN IN THE WORLD!

© 1981 United Feature Syndicate, Inc.

LAWRENCE & MORROW 1-20

I-I'M SORRY... THERE'S NOTHING I CAN DO ABOUT THAT!

AH, BUT THERE'S SOMETHING YOU COULD DO FOR ME --IF YOU WOULD!

36

YOU KNOW HOW LADY LAWLEY PREENS HERSELF ON BEING THE SMARTEST WHIP IN THE *BEAU MONDE?*

SHE HAS WON MANY RACES IN HER CURRICLE!

NEVERTHELESS, I COULD NOT STAND HER BOASTING-- ESPECIALLY AFTER SEEING HOW WELL *YOU* DROVE IN THE PARK!

SO I BET HER FAR MORE THAN I CAN AFFORD-- THAT I KNEW A YOUNG LADY WHO COULD *BEAT* HER HANDS DOWN!

YOU ARE ASKING ME TO RACE AGAINST LADY LAWLEY?!

UNLESS YOU COME TO MY RESCUE, THERE IS NO WAY I CAN MAKE GOOD ON MY BET!

V-VERY WELL ...I--I ONLY HOPE I SHAN'T LET YOU DOWN!

OH, MY DEAR-- THAT IS IMPOSSIBLE! I KNEW YOU WOULD NOT FAIL ME!

That afternoon, the Earl attends a boxing match in Chiswick...

WHAT A BRUTE I WAS TO TAKE OUT MY TEMPER ON PETRINA!

Lord Rowlock calls for Petrina...

LUCKILY, MY CHAPERON, THE DUCHESS, IS ASLEEP! ...WHAT IS TO BE THE STARTING POINT FOR THE RACE?

WE FROM TYBURN-- LADY LAWLEY FROM PORTMAN SQUARE! EACH ON OUR HONOR TO LEAVE NOT A SECOND BEFORE ONE O'CLOCK!

LAWRENCE & MORROW

Meanwhile, as the Earl starts back to London...

NO WONDER ISOLDA SEEMED SO SURE OF HERSELF THE OTHER NIGHT!... EXCEPT FOR PETRINA, SHE WOULD HAVE TRAPPED ME NEATLY!

1/23

WHAT ABOUT OUR DESTINATION?

AN INN CALLED THE PLUME OF FEATHERS-- OFF THE GREAT NORTH ROAD!

1/24

WE'VE NO WAY OF KNOWING WHETHER LADY LAWLEY IS AHEAD OF US OR BEHIND US!

LAWRENCE & MORROW

DO NOT FRET, MY DEAR! YOU SHALL LEARN THE OUTCOME OF OUR LITTLE ADVENTURE SOON ENOUGH, WHEN WE REACH THE INN!

As Petrina and Lord Rowlock reach the Plume of Feathers...

HAS ANOTHER CURRICLE ARRIVED --DRIVEN BY A LADY?

NO, SIR.!

THEN WE'VE DONE IT.! WE'VE WON THE RACE!

TO THE MOST MAGNIFICENT DRIVER--AND ONE SO BEAUTIFUL, WORDS CANNOT EXPRESS HOW MUCH I LOVE HER!

Y-YOU MUST NOT SAY SUCH THINGS! YOU KNOW HOW ANGRY MY GUARDIAN WOULD BE!

OH--I MUST HAVE FALLEN ASLEEP! YOU SHOULD HAVE WAKENED ME!... WHAT TIME IS IT?

NEARLY FIVE O'CLOCK..., BUT YOU LOOKED SO LOVELY, MY DEAR --AND YOU NEEDED THE REST!

WE MUST GO AT ONCE! WHAT ON EARTH IS KEEPING LADY LAWLEY?

AN ACCIDENT, PERHAPS--OR PIQUE AT LOSING! NO MATTER-- I WILL ORDER THE CURRICLE!

Presently--

WELL?

ONE OF THE HORSES HAS DROPPED A SHOE!

39

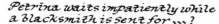
Petrina waits impatiently while a blacksmith is sent for ...?

OH DEAR! THE EARL WILL BE FURIOUS WHEN HE LEARNS WHERE I HAVE BEEN!

© 1981 United Feature Syndicate, Inc.

IS NOT THE SMITH HERE YET?

THE GROOM SAYS HE WAS NOT AT HIS FORGE, BUT IS EXPECTED SOON... LET US HAVE SOME REFRESHMENT, MY DEAR!

While ...
PETRINA WENT DRIVING, YOU SAY? WITH WHOM?

I REGRET TO SAY, M'LORD--THE FOOTMAN DID NOT RECOGNIZE THE GENTLEMAN WHO CALLED FOR HER!

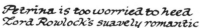
Petrina is too worried to heed Lord Rowlock's suavely romantic compliments ...

OH PLEASE! DO GO AND SEE IF THE BLACKSMITH HAS ARRIVED!

WE DO NOT NEED ANY MORE TO DRINK!

THE GENTLEMAN ORDERED THE PORT, MA'AM!

© 1981 United Feature Syndicate, Inc.

WELL? WHAT IS WRONG?... SURELY HE IS HERE BY NOW!

NO, MY DEAR-- I AM AFRAID YOU MUST RESIGN YOURSELF TO STAYING A WHILE LONGER!

40

41

Desperately Petrina tries to send off Lord Rowlock's brutal advances!

IT'S TOO LATE FOR WORDS, MY DEAR! ... SURELY YOU CANNOT BLAME ME FOR WISHING TO EMBRACE MY FUTURE WIFE?

NO! ... STAY AWAY FROM ME!!

Moments later, she bursts out of the inn ... and by luck finds a chaise waiting in the yard!

IS SOMETHING WRONG, MISS?!

THERE'S BEEN AN ACCIDENT! YOUR MASTER NEEDS YOU! ... GO SEE TO HIM! I'LL HOLD THE REINS!

PETRINA! ... WHAT HAS HAPPENED?!

I-I HAVE KILLED A MAN! ... AND STOLEN A CHAISE!

Trembling, Petrina tells how Lord Rowlock tricked her ... how she fought to save herself ... then fled from the inn!

OH P-PLEASE --DON'T LEAVE ME!

DON'T BE FRIGHTENED, MY DEAR-- JUST REST! I WILL GO BACK TO THE INN AND ATTEND TO EVERYTHING!

Far from resting, Petrina finds her heart beating faster than ever when the Earl has gone!

HE KISSED ME! ...PERHAPS IT WAS ONLY TO COMFORT ME, BUT--OH, I LOVE HIM SO MUCH!

NEVER MIND! I C-CANNOT STAY HERE...I HAVE KILLED A MAN! I MUST FIND SOME PLACE TO HIDE!

--ELSE THEY WILL SEND ME TO NEWGATE--TO BE HANGED OR TRANSPORTED!

Meanwhile...

WHAT A FOOL I'VE BEEN!...NO WONDER ISOLDA AND LA VOUVRAY MEANT SO LITTLE TO ME-- ONCE PETRINA CAME INTO MY LIFE!

The Earl asks at the inn if anyone has lost a chaise...

AYE! MINE WAS STOLEN, SIR!

THEN I HAVE THE PLEASURE OF RETURNING IT! I FOUND IT BY THE ROAD-- WITH YOUR HORSES CROPPING GRASS!

'TWAS TAKEN BY A DOXY WHO CAME HERE WITH LORD ROWLOCK! STABBED HIM, SHE DID-- THEN RAN OFF!

SURGEON SAYS HE'LL NEED NURSING FOR A SPELL 'FORE HE'S UP AND ABOUT!

HOW VERY INCONVENIENT! BUT I FEEL SURE YOU'LL LOOK AFTER HIM WELL!

Taking his steward's key--Petrina has gone to the house in Paradise Row that the Earl formerly lent to Mlle. Vouvray...

AT LEAST I CAN HIDE HERE FOR A WHILE--!

--EVEN IF HE NEVER WANTS TO SEE ME AGAIN B-BECAUSE OF ALL THE SCANDAL I CAUSED!

PETRINA--!

OH! IT IS YOU!...Y-YOU CAME TO FIND ME!

TO TELL YOU THAT YOU HAVE NOTHING TO FEAR--AND BRING YOU HOME, MY LOVE!

YOU CALLED ME ... 'MY LOVE!'

OF COURSE! HOW ELSE SHOULD I ADDRESS THE LOVELY CREATURE WHO I HOPE WILL BECOME MY WIFE!

YOU CANNOT MEAN THAT?! NOT AFTER ALL THE TROUBLE I HAVE CAUSED YOU, AS YOUR WARD!

BUT I DO MEAN IT!

... THERE IS NO ONE SO UNPREDICTABLE AND INCORRIGIBLE --YET I WOULD NOT HAVE YOU OTHERWISE, MY PRECIOUS PETRINA!

44

The End

Barbara Cartland
PICTURE ROMANCES

THE ARCHDUKE FERDINAND WISHES TO SEE YOU IN HIS STUDY, YOUR ROYAL HIGHNESS.

ZOSINA! WAKE UP! PAPA WISHES TO SEE YOU!

WHAT?

YOU HAD BETTER HURRY! YOU KNOW HOW PAPA IS.

I AM GLAD HE DID NOT SEND FOR ME!

GOOD LUCK!

WHAT CAN I HAVE DONE TO UPSET PAPA NOW? IT IS NOT MY FAULT I WAS NOT BORN A BOY!

PAPA? YOU WISHED TO SEE ME?

AH, ZOSINA. SIT DOWN. I HAVE SOME EXTREMELY GOOD NEWS FOR YOU, MY DEAR. IT IS GRATIFYING, VERY GRATIFYING THAT THE NEGOTIATIONS OF OUR AMBASSADOR SHOULD PROVE SO FRUITFUL.

NEGOTIATIONS?

YES, IT IS ALL ARRANGED. YOU ARE TO BE MARRIED AS SOON AS POSSIBLE TO KING GYORGY OF DORSIA.

MARRIED!

MARRIED? BUT... I HAVE NEVER EVEN **MET** THE KING!

IT IS A POLITICAL MARRIAGE.

IN ORDER FOR DORSIA AND LÜTZELSTEIN TO MAINTAIN INDEPENDENCE FROM GERMANY, THERE MUST BE AN OFFICIAL ALLIANCE BETWEEN OUR TWO COUNTRIES.

BUT PAPA, SUPPOSE THE KING... DISLIKES ME, AND I **DISLIKE HIM**?

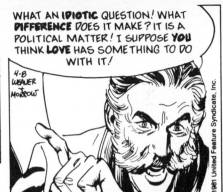

WHAT AN **IDIOTIC** QUESTION! WHAT **DIFFERENCE** DOES IT MAKE? IT IS A POLITICAL MATTER! I SUPPOSE **YOU** THINK **LOVE** HAS SOMETHING TO DO WITH IT!

4-8 WEAVER & MORROW

© 1981 United Feature Syndicate, Inc.

THE DECISION IS **FINAL**! YOUR MARRIAGE TO KING GYORGY HAS BEEN ARRANGED!

BUT... SHOULD I NOT **MEET** THE KING BEFORE--

WEAVER & MORROW 4/9

OF COURSE YOU WILL MEET! YOU ARE TO PAY A STATE VISIT TO DORSIA WITH YOUR GRANDMOTHER, THE QUEEN MOTHER. IF I DID NOT HAVE THIS BAD LEG I WOULD GO WITH YOU MYSELF.

© 1981 United Feature Syndicate, Inc.

WHY WAS I CURSED WITH **THREE DAUGHTERS**? UNGRATEFUL AND HALF-WITTED TO BOOT!

© 1981 United Feature Syndicate, Inc.

The royal train arrives in Dorsia to cheering crowds, who realize the importance of the political alliance....

WEAVER & MORROW

HIS MAJESTY, KING GYORGY. HER ROYAL HIGHNESS, THE PRINCESS ZOSINA.

© 1981 United Feature Syndicate, Inc.

WELCOME TO DORSIA.

I KNEW IT! HE DOES **NOT LIKE** ME.

4-13

HE RESENTS ME. HE DOES NOT **WISH** TO MARRY ME.

THE KING'S UNCLE, YOUR HIGHNESS — THE REGENT, PRINCE SANDOR.

IT IS ALWAYS BEWILDERING TO MEET SO MANY NEW PEOPLE, BUT I ASSURE YOU THEY ARE AS DELIGHTED TO SEE YOU AS I AM.

THANK YOU, YOU ARE VERY KIND.

WEAVER & MORROW

AT LEAST *SOMEONE* IS GLAD TO SEE ME ...BUT I EXPECTED THE REGENT TO BE MUCH OLDER.

© 1981 United Feature Syndicate, Inc.

4-14

I THINK, SIRE, YOUR PALACE MUST BE THE MOST BEAUTIFUL IN ALL OF EUROPE.

REALLY? I INTEND TO HAVE IT REDECORATED AS SOON AS POSSIBLE.

OH, BUT—

IF YOU THINK YOU ARE GOING TO INTERFERE WITH MY PLANS JUST BECAUSE OF THIS MARRIAGE IDEA, YOU ARE SADLY **MISTAKEN**.

HE THINKS I SHALL TRY TO STOP HIM FROM ENJOYING HIMSELF. HE DISLIKED ME EVEN BEFORE WE MET. WHAT WILL I **DO**?

4-15

© 1981 United Feature Syndicate, Inc.

I HEARD YOU ADMIRING THE PALACE. I AM GLAD YOU LIKE IT.

IT IS LOVELY! AS IS DORSIA ITSELF. ONLY POETRY WOULD BE ADEQUATE TO DESCRIBE IT.

POETRY IS RATHER LIKE MUSIC, IS IT NOT? IT CAN OFTEN EXPRESS WHAT ORDINARY WORDS CANNOT.

YES! YES, EXACTLY. I AM AFRAID HIS MAJESTY MISUNDERSTOOD ME.

4-16 WEAVER & MORROW

YOU ARE FOND OF POETRY?

OH, VERY!

SO AM I.

© 1981 United Feature Syndicate, Inc.

THERE ARE SO MANY CURIOUS EYES ON YOU TWO, I THOUGHT I WOULD LEAVE YOU **ALONE** TO GET TO KNOW EACH OTHER.

BUT GRANDMAMA...

WE WILL FORGET PROTOCOL FOR THE MOMENT. NOW TALK TO EACH OTHER.

GRANDMAMA ALWAYS TRIES TO MAKE THINGS EASIER...

I SEE NOTHING **EASY** ABOUT YOUR BEING HERE... **OR** THIS WRETCHED MARRIAGE!

4-17

I DID NOT WISH TO GET MARRIED EITHER, BUT FOR POLITICAL REASONS—

YOU EXPECT ME TO **BELIEVE THAT**? EVERY WOMAN WANTS A CROWN ON HER HEAD.

YOU ARE BEING NEEDLESSLY INSULTING.

DO NOT WORRY. ONCE WE ARE MARRIED, SINCE WE HAVE TO...

...YOU MAY GO **YOUR** WAY AND I WILL GO **MINE**!

HE'S BEHAVING LIKE A SPOILED SCHOOLBOY! HOW CAN I MARRY ANYBODY LIKE **THAT**?

4-18

54

YOUR MAJESTY, THIS WOULD BE A LOVELY ROOM IN WHICH TO DANCE. DO YOU EVER GIVE BALLS AT THE PALACE?

THE PALACE BALLS ARE ALWAYS BORING.

I AM SURE YOU HAVE MANY FRIENDS WHO ENJOY DANCING AS I DO.

MY FRIENDS ARE **NOT GOOD ENOUGH** FOR THE REGENT. THEY NEVER COME HERE.

SO I AM FORCED TO GO TO THEM. WOULD YOU LIKE TO ACCOMPANY ME?

© 1981 United Feature Syndicate, Inc.

THERE IS A MASKED BALL IN THE VILLAGE TONIGHT. WE CAN SLIP **OUT** WHEN EVERYONE HAS GONE TO BED.

LEAVE THE PALACE?

I **KNEW** YOU WERE NOT BRAVE ENOUGH TO COME.

I DID NOT **SAY** THAT! I **WILL** COME, IF YOU CAN MAKE CERTAIN NO ONE WILL FIND OUT.

LEAVE EVERYTHING TO ME. BE READY.

WHAT AM I *DOING*?

© 1981 United Feature Syndicate, Inc.

Late that night, Zosina awaits the King's signal... 4-24

WEAVER & MORROW

OH! I DID NOT HEAR YOU KNOCK.

I DIDN'T KNOCK! COME WITH ME. KING GYORGY IS WAITING. AND TRY TO BE QUIET!

WHERE ARE YOU TAKING ME?

TO THE PALACE CELLARS. DO NOT WORRY. EXCEPT FOR THE RATS, THERE IS NO ONE DOWN THERE.

© 1981 United Feature Syndicate, Inc.

WHERE HAVE YOU BEEN? I THOUGHT YOU WERE GOING TO GIVE ME AWAY.

OF COURSE NOT!

PUT THESE ON. NO ONE WILL RECOGNIZE EITHER OF US.

THIS IS RATHER EXCITING!

COME QUICKLY. MY FRIENDS ARE WAITING. NOW THE FUN CAN BEGIN!

© 1981 United Feature Syndicate, Inc.

WEAVER & MORROW 4-25

59

TELL ME THE TRUTH... DO **YOU** LOVE **ME**, TOO?

OF COURSE I LOVE YOU. EVER SINCE I FIRST SET EYES ON YOU.

BUT YOU MUST MARRY **THE KING**, FOR THE INDEPENDENCE OF DORSIA AND LUTZELSTEIN. YOU **KNOW** THAT, ZOSINA.

EVEN NOW THAT WE HAVE **FOUND** EACH OTHER?

LOEWER & MORROW 5-8

IT IS **TOO LATE!** THERE IS NOTHING TO SAY... EXCEPT **GOODBYE.**

© 1981 United Feature Syndicate, Inc.

GO STRAIGHT ALONG THIS PASSAGE AND YOU WILL SEE A STAIRCASE WHICH WILL LEAD YOU TO YOUR ROOM. WE MUST **NOT** BE **SEEN** TOGETHER, MY DARLING.

FOR **YOUR** SAKE, AND FOR THE SAKE OF OUR **COUNTRIES**, I WILL MARRY THE KING...

BUT IT IS **YOU** I LOVE.

LOEWER & MORROW 5/9

© 1981 United Feature Syndicate, Inc.

62

...A SLEEPLESS NIGHT....

HOW CAN ANY MAN, LET ALONE A KING, FIND THAT SORT OF BEHAVIOR ENJOYABLE?

HIS **WIFE**! HOW CAN I BE HIS WIFE WHEN I LOATHE AND DESPISE HIM? WHAT CAN I DO? WHAT CAN I **DO**?

I CANNOT **BREATHE** IN HERE. I MUST GET SOME **AIR** ...

DAWN AT THE ROYAL STABLES...

I AM GOING RIDING. PLEASE SADDLE ME A HORSE.

YES, YOUR HIGHNESS.

THIS IS THE HORSE I WISH TO RIDE.

BUT YOUR HIGHNESS, I THINK THIS STALLION WILL BE **TOO MUCH** FOR YOU. HIS NAME IS SAMU. HE BELONGS TO THE **REGENT**.

I WISH TO RIDE SAMU. SURELY THE REGENT WILL NOT MIND.

VERY GOOD, YOUR HIGHNESS.

SO SAMU IS THE REGENT'S HORSE... I MIGHT HAVE GUESSED.

NIKI WILL GO AS YOUR GROOM, YOUR HIGHNESS, ON ANOTHER HORSE.

OH, THAT WON'T BE NECESSARY—

IT IS **SAFER**. THERE ARE **GYPSIES** IN THE MOUNTAINS.

VERY WELL.

WE CROSS THE RIVER HERE, AND YOU'LL BE IN THE WILD COUNTRY BELOW THE MOUNTAINS, AND—

WHY MUST HE **CHATTER** SO? I CAN HARDLY **THINK**!

THIS COUNTRYSIDE IS WONDERFUL FOR HORSES, AND—

I CANNOT **BEAR** IT! I MUST BE **ALONE**! I MUST **THINK**!

MY HANDKERCHIEF! I HAVE DROPPED IT!

I'LL FETCH IT FOR YOUR ROYAL HIGHNESS.

YOUR **HIGHNESS**!

WEAVER + MORROW 5-16

I KNOW I MUST TURN BACK. THEY WILL BE WORRIED...

BUT I CANNOT **GO BACK**! I CANNOT GO BACK WHEN I **LOVE** THE **REGENT** AND I MUST **MARRY** THE KING!

IT MUST BE ALMOST NOON, AND I'VE BEEN RIDING SINCE DAWN. I'M SO THIRSTY, AS I'M SURE YOU ARE, SAMU. I WILL LOOK FOR A PLACE TO STOP.

GYPSIES! BUT THERE ARE CHILDREN WITH THEM. THEY DO NOT **LOOK** DANGEROUS.

THIS TEA IS WONDERFUL!

PEOPLE ARE **WRONG** ABOUT GYPSIES...

THEY ARE VERY KIND.

HOW ARE YOU FEELING, MY DARLING?

IN A WAY I AM SORRY I REGAINED CONSCIOUSNESS...

..BECAUSE I KNOW I SHALL HAVE TO RETURN TO MARRY THE KING.

PLEASE DO NOT TORTURE ME, ZOSINA! I CANNOT BEAR TO THINK OF YOU WITH HIM!

NEVER MIND. I KNOW THERE IS NO CHOICE. MEANWHILE IT WILL BE WONDERFUL TO RIDE WITH YOU THROUGH THIS BEAUTIFUL COUNTRY-SIDE.

MY DARLING...

WEAVER & MORROW © 1981 United Feature Syndicate, Inc. 5/25

I WILL LEAVE DORSIA BEFORE YOUR WEDDING.

BUT WHAT WILL I DO WITHOUT YOU?

WHERE WILL YOU GO?

ANYWHERE ... JUST SO I DO NOT HAVE TO WATCH YOU WITH HIM!

WHEN I WAS A LITTLE GIRL, I THOUGHT DREAMS CAME TRUE. I THOUGHT YOU MARRIED THE MAN YOU LOVED. I BELIEVED THE POETRY I READ... BUT I WAS WRONG!!

WEAVER & MORROW 5/26 © 1981 United Feature Syndicate, Inc.

WHEN WE REACH THE END OF THIS CORRIDOR I WILL SAY GOODBYE TO YOU FOREVER.

MY DARLING—

OH, DO NOT SAY IT!

SIRE! YOU HAVE RETURNED! THE PRIME MINISTER WISHES TO SEE YOU IMMEDIATELY, WITH THE PRINCESS ZOSINA, IN THE SALON.

CAN HE KNOW ABOUT...US?

LET ME HANDLE IT.

YOU WISHED TO SPEAK WITH ME?

IT IS WITH DEEP REGRET, SIRE, THAT I BRING YOU BAD NEWS.

BAD NEWS?

HIS MAJESTY, KING GYORGY, WAS INVOLVED IN A RIOT IN THE VILLAGE LAST NIGHT. HE WAS HIT WITH A PIECE OF FLYING GLASS AND WAS KILLED INSTANTLY!

KING GYORGY IS DEAD, THE SUCCESSION PASSES TO YOU! LONG LIVE THE KING!

After a suitable period of mourning, Zosina and the new King are married...

AM I **REALLY** MARRYING YOU, OR AM I **DREAMING**?

IT IS **REAL**, MY DARLING.

REMEMBER WHAT YOU SAID ABOUT DREAMS COMING **TRUE**?

OH, YES!

I NOW PRONOUNCE YOU **MAN** AND **WIFE**.

LONG LIVE THE KING! LONG LIVE THE QUEEN!

THIS IS OUR COUNTRY, DEAREST. WE HAVE **UNITED** DORSIA AND LÜTZELSTIEN AND SECURED THEIR INDEPENDENCE FROM THE GERMAN EMPIRE.

AND DO YOU KNOW WHAT ELSE WE HAVE DONE?

WHAT IS THAT?

WE ARE UNITED, YOU AND I, AND **WE WILL NEVER BE PARTED.**

The End

Barbara Cartland
PICTURE ROMANCES

The Treasure Is Love

After thirteen years in India fighting Napoleon, Tyson Dale returns to Revel Royal, his glorious family estate. Something is different, however...

WEAVER & MORROW 2/9

© 1981 United Feature Syndicate, Inc.

HELLO! IS THERE NO ONE HERE?

MASTER TYSON!

MRS. BRIGGS! THANK THE LORD! I THOUGHT THE HOUSE WAS DESERTED!

© 1981 United Feature Syndicate, Inc.

NO, I BE HERE WITH MR. BRIGGS, BUT WE'RE THE ONLY ONES, SIR.

I DON'T UNDERSTAND ...WHERE ARE THE REST OF THE SERVANTS?

THEY ALL LEFT WHEN YOUR FATHER DIED, SIR. THERE WAS NO MONEY.

NO MONEY! WHAT HAPPENED TO MY FATHER'S FORTUNE?!

WEAVER & MORROW 2/10

I'LL BE MAKING UP THE MASTER BEDROOM FOR YOU, SIR, IF THE CEILING HASN'T FALLEN FROM THE DAMP. I'M GLAD YOU'RE HOME, MASTER TYSON.

NOW REVEL ROYAL WILL RETURN TO THE WAY IT WAS WHEN YOUR DEAR MOTHER WAS ALIVE. YOU'LL PUT IT TO RIGHTS NOW, SIR.

HOW CAN I RESTORE REVEL ROYAL TO ITS RIGHTFUL SPLENDOR WHEN I MYSELF HAVE BARELY ENOUGH TO FEED MY HORSE ...

WHAT COULD HAVE HAPPENED? MOTHER ... IF ONLY YOU WERE HERE ...

LOOK WHAT I SHOT FOR YOU, MOTHER!

YOU ARE THE BRAVEST LITTLE MAN I KNOW, AND ONE DAY, WHEN YOU ARE LORD WELLINGDALE AND OWNER OF REVEL ROYAL, YOU WILL BE THE BRAVEST MAN IN THE WORLD.

FOR YOU, MOTHER, I WILL BE THE BRAVEST. I WILL FIND OUT WHAT DISASTER HAS BEFALLEN REVEL ROYAL AND I WILL SET IT TO RIGHTS.

© 1981 United Feature Syndicate, Inc.

After learning the bad news about his family's fortune, Tyson Dale stops at his favorite Inn for a rejuvenating glass of imported claret... 3/16

WHERE'S OLD TUG?

SOLD THE PLACE YEARS AGO, MATE. YOU NEW IN TOWN?

WEAVER+ MORROW

NEW?... EVERYTHING'S CHANGED. I'D BEST BE SADDLING SALAMANCA AND GETTING BACK TO REVEL ROYAL BEFORE THIS CLARET FOGS MY MIND COMPLETELY.

I DOPED THE OLD COUPLE'S WINE. HAVE YOU GIVEN THE COACHMEN ENOUGH TO KEEP THEM QUIET?

2/17

In the Inn's stable...

DON'T YE WORRY, GUV'NOR, THEY'LL SLEEP LOIK LOGS TILL MORNIN'.

WEAVER + MORROW

AND TAKE CARE YOU BRING ALL THE YOUNG LADY'S LUGGAGE DOWN AFTER ME. I'M TAKING **EVERYTHING** I CAN GET.

RIGHT, SIR NEVILLE.

SHE MAY STRUGGLE, SO MIND YOU HAVE THE COACH READY TO LEAVE IMMEDIATELY. **NO ONE** MUST STOP US!

79

80

81

After Tyson saves the girl from "a fate worse than death", they hurriedly leave the Dog and Duck...

WEAVER 2/23 MORROW

LET US GO QUICKLY BEFORE THEY DISCOVER I HAVE GONE!

WE'LL TAKE THIS COACH. IT IS PROBABLY THE ONE IN WHICH HE PLANNED TO CARRY YOU OFF, ANYWAY. MY HORSE WILL FOLLOW US.

PLEASE **HURRY!**

OH ... IT IS **LOVELY** ...

AS YOU SEE, IT IS IN SOME NEED OF REPAIR ... BUT I DO NOT INTEND TO APOLOGIZE FOR ITS SHORTCOMINGS.

OF COURSE NOT.

TONIGHT, YOU WILL SLEEP IN MY MOTHER'S ROOM. TOMORROW IS TIME ENOUGH TO DISCUSS YOUR SITUATION. EVERYTHING WILL SEEM BETTER AFTER A GOOD REST.

I ... I AM TIRED ...

AND NO WONDER.

WEAVER & MORROW 2/24

I NEVER THOUGHT ANYONE COULD BE SO ... UNEXPECTEDLY WONDERFUL TO A STRANGER ...

NOW, THEN. YOU KNOW THAT YOU CANNOT STAY HERE WITH ME **ALONE**. AS SOON AS POSSIBLE YOU MUST GO TO A RELATION OR A FRIEND WHOM YOU CAN TRUST. WHAT IS YOUR UNCLE'S NAME?

NO.

NO?

MY NAME IS VANIA ... BUT THAT IS **ALL** I WILL TELL YOU.

2/25
WEAVER
+
MORROW

I HAVE DECIDED TO REMAIN **HERE** AND HELP YOU PUT YOUR HOUSE IN ORDER.

© 1981 United Feature Syndicate, Inc.

DASH IT, YOU ARE BEING DELIBERATELY OBSTRUCTIVE. YOU MUST FACE FACTS, UNPALATABLE THOUGH THEY MAY BE. CONSIDER YOUR **REPUTATION**.

IF MY REPUTATION DOESN'T CONCERN **ME**, IT NEEDN'T CONCERN **YOU**!

LET US STOP PLAY-ACTING. TELL ME YOUR UNCLE'S NAME.

IT IS AMAZING. YOU SOUND **EXACTLY** LIKE MY SCHOOLMISTRESS.

2/26

WEAVER
MORROW

I THINK YOU NEED A GOOD **SPANKING**! I INSIST THAT--

OH, LET'S CALL A TRUCE FOR NOW! I WANT TO EXPLORE REVEL ROYAL!

© 1981 United Feature Syndicate, Inc.

84

86

SO YOU KNOW **NOTHING** ABOUT THE GIRL?

OF COURSE NOT.

YOU UNDERSTAND MY POSITION. SHE IS **VERY RICH**. I CANNOT LET ALL THAT MONEY SLIP THROUGH MY FINGERS... I HAVE A LITTLE MISTRESS WHO LIKES DIAMONDS...

EVEN IF I **COULD** HELP YOU, YOU MAY BE SURE I WOULD **NOT**.

I SEE YOUR QUESTIONABLE BIRTH IS REVEALED ALSO BY YOUR NATURE, SIR!

LEAVE IMMEDIATELY, SIR!

UNDOUBTEDLY YOU ARE ANGRY BECAUSE I SPEAK THE TRUTH.

MY FATHER IS LORD WELLINGDALE BECAUSE YOUR PARENTS WERE NEVER UNITED IN MATRIMONY.

I DO NOT WISH TO DISCUSS IT WITH YOU.

MY, MY. I SUGGEST YOU DO SOMETHING ABOUT THIS HOUSE WITH THE MONEY YOU HAVE LEFT. IT **IS** IN BAD SHAPE, IS IT NOT?

YOU MAY TELL YOUR FATHER, SIR, THAT I INTEND TO **CHALLENGE** HIS RIGHT TO THE TITLE OF LORD WELLINGDALE.

THEY SAY A BRITISH SOLDIER NEVER KNOWS WHEN HE IS **BEATEN**...

BUT KEEP YOUR OPTIMISM, SIR; YOU DO NOT HAVE MUCH **ELSE**.

REST ASSURED THAT ONCE MY HEIRESS IS FOUND, I SHALL NOT INVITE YOU TO THE WEDDING, GOOD DAY.

© 1981 United Feature Syndicate, Inc.

SO...HE IS YOUR COUSIN,

AND **YOU** ARE AN HEIRESS.

NOW YOU SEE WHY I CANNOT MARRY HIM. HE IS DESPICABLE.

YES. OF COURSE.

BUT NOW THAT I KNOW YOUR IDENTITY I AM OBLIGED TO COMMUNICATE YOUR WHEREABOUTS TO YOUR UNCLE.

WHY?! **WHY**?! PLEASE DO NOT SEND ME AWAY!

© 1981 United Feature Syndicate, Inc.

I WANT TO HELP YOU FIND PROOF THAT YOUR PARENTS WERE MARRIED, AND TO FIND YOUR FATHER'S FORTUNE!

NO!

I KNOW WE WILL FIND IT SOMEWHERE IN REVEL ROYAL! OH, PLEASE...

TOMORROW MORNING I WILL TAKE YOU TO A ROADSIDE INN! NO ONE NEED KNOW YOU WERE HERE.

WEAVER & MORROW

YOU WILL FORCE ME INTO MARRIAGE WITH YOUR COUSIN?

WHAT ELSE ARE WE TO DO?

© 1981 United Feature Syndicate, Inc.

LET ME STAY.

I HAVE TOLD YOU THAT THAT IS IMPOSSIBLE!

I COULD SUGGEST A WAY IT WOULD BE POSSIBLE...

HOW?

YOU COULD MARRY ME!

WEAVER & MORROW 3-14

© 1981 United Feature Syndicate, Inc.

TELL THE TRUTH,... TELL ME THE *REAL* REASON YOU WILL NOT MARRY ME!

VANIA... I HAVE NOTHING TO OFFER YOU.

AND BEING A MAN OF HONOR, I FIND IT IMPOSSIBLE TO ACT LIKE A CAD.

IF... WE PROVED YOUR PARENTS WERE MARRIED, **THEN** WOULD YOU MARRY ME?

I CANNOT ANSWER SUCH A HYPOTHETICAL QUESTION.

WEAVER & MORROW

© 1981 United Feature Syndicate, Inc.

3/16

Meanwhile, at the Dog and Duck...

GUV'NOR, YOU WAS ASKIN' ABOUT WHO WAS 'ERE TUESDAY LAST? THE NIGHT OF THE KIDNAPPIN'?

YES?

I JUST REMEMBERED SOMEONE ELSE, HE DRANK A BOTTLE OF OUR BEST CLARET--

WHO? OUT WITH IT!

IT WAS TYSON DALE, GUV'NOR, THE MASTER OF REVEL ROYAL.

TYSON WAS HERE, WAS HE?

WEAVER + MORROW 3/17

© 1981 United Feature Syndicate, Inc.

91

I'VE HIRED A CARRIAGE FOR TOMORROW MORNING

OH, **NO**...

TYSON, WILL YOU SHOW ME YOUR MOTHER'S ROSE GARDEN?

YOU MUST KNOW BY NOW THAT I LOVE YOU WITH ALL MY HEART. YOU ARE TOO PROUD TO ADMIT IT, BUT I THINK YOU LOVE ME TOO...

© 1981 United Feature Syndicate, Inc.

VANIA...I **DO** LOVE YOU--

BUT WE CAN NEVER BE TOGETHER.

YOU DO! OH, I **KNEW** IT! OH, TYSON!

YOU WOULD SACRIFICE ME TO YOUR **PRINCIPLES**? TYSON ...LET US BE ADVENTUROUS! LET US BELONG TO EACH OTHER! NOTHING ELSE MATTERS!

VANIA...I LOVE YOU...BUT MY PRINCIPLES ARE ALL I HAVE. YOU **MUST** GO!

ALL RIGHT, TYSON. I UNDER-STAND. AND I LOVE YOU FOR BEING A MAN OF HONOR.

VANIA...

I WILL RETURN TO MY UNCLE. BUT I AM **YOURS**, YOURS **COMPLETELY** FROM NOW UNTIL ETERNITY.

© 1981 United Feature Syndicate, Inc.

96

HELLO, MY SLEEPING BEAUTY.

OH, TYSON... I CANNOT BELIEVE I AM REALLY HERE WITH YOU... I HAD A DREAM ABOUT YOUR MOTHER JUST NOW... WHEN DID SHE DIE?

CLOSE UPON THE DEATH OF MY FATHER ... I THINK HER HEART WAS BROKEN.

IN MY DREAM SHE WAS HOLDING A BOOK, AND SHOWING IT TO ME,

A SMALL BOOK ... LIKE A DIARY?

YES! A DIARY.

HMM. MY MOTHER DID KEEP A DIARY. I WONDER ...VANIA! DO YOU SUPPOSE WE MIGHT FIND A CLUE ...?

JUNE 16, 1782 ... VANIA, LISTEN TO THIS!

"...It is perfectly Right and Legal for the Captain of a Ship to Marry any of his Passengers. Hubert took my hand, the Captain had his Prayer-Book ready, and we were Married!"

OH, TYSON! THE PROOF!

IT IS NOT JUST TYSON ANY LONGER. IT IS LORD WELLINGDALE. AND YOU, MY PRECIOUS, ARE LADY WELLINGDALE.

The End

Barbara Cartland

PICTURE ROMANCES

YOU KNOW, MY BOY, YOU ARE SUPPOSED TO **ENJOY** THIS TRIP TO SCOTLAND WITH THE KING, BUT YOU'VE BEEN SCOWLING FOR DAYS!

~Beginning~
The Chieftain Without a Heart

YOU KNOW QUITE WELL, LORD HINCHLEY, THAT I LEFT SCOTLAND AT AGE SIXTEEN AND VOWED **NEVER** TO RETURN. BUT THERE IS SOMETHING YOU DO *NOT* KNOW...

WEAVER & MORROW 6/1

LAST WEEK I WAS SUMMONED BACK BY MY CLAN, OF WHICH, LORD HINCHLEY, I AM NOW *CHIEFTAIN*.

CHIEFTAIN?!

I WISH THE ROYAL VISIT WITH THE KING *WERE* THE ONLY REASON I WAS RETURNING TO SCOTLAND.

I CANNOT BELIEVE *YOU* ARE THE CHIEFTAIN OF THE McNARNS.

I WISH IT WERE **NOT** SO. A CRISIS HAS ARISEN, AND I HAVE BEEN SUMMONED TO SCOTLAND TO DEAL WITH IT.

THE CLAN SEEMS **DETERMINED** TO *FORCE* ME TO ACKNOWLEDGE MY HERITAGE.

WEAVER-MORROW

SO I MUST LEAVE THE SHIP HERE, AND SEE YOU AND THE KING IN EDINBURGH IN A FEW DAYS.

IS THERE SOMEONE TO MEET YOU?

YES, THOSE MEN DOWN THERE ARE WEARING THE TARTANS OF THE **MCNARN** CLAN.

FRANKLY, I **ENVY** YOU, OLD BOY! I THINK IT IS RATHER *THRILLING!*

DO NOT WASTE YOUR ENVY ON **ME**. I WILL BE **AWAY** FROM HERE AS **SOON** AS I *POSSIBLY* **CAN!**

WELCOME. WE HAVE BEEN WAITING EAGERLY FOR YOUR RETURN,—

THANK YOU—

BUT I WILL *NOT* BE STAYING LONG.

THE MCNARNS HAD HOPED THAT AS THE NEW CHIEF-TAIN YOU WOULD **REMAIN** TO LEAD THE CLAN.

I AM AFRAID THAT IS *IMPOSSIBLE.* PLEASE TELL ME WHAT CRISIS HAS OCCURRED SO THAT I MAY **DEAL** WITH IT AND BE **OFF.**

YOUR NEPHEW, TORQUIL McNARN, WAS CAUGHT STEALING CATTLE FROM THE **KILCRAIG** CLAN. THEY ARE HOLDING HIM **PRISONER** NOW.

I FEEL AS IF I HAD STEPPED INTO THE **PAST.**

IT IS VERY SERIOUS.

YOU KNOW WHAT BITTER *RIVALS* THE McNARNS AND THE KILCRAIGS ARE.

THIS IS INTOLERABLE. WE WILL SETTLE THE MATTER WITH THE CHIEFTAIN OF THE KILCRAIGS OVER A GLASS OF PORT, LIKE *GENTLEMEN!*

WEAVER & MORROW

WE HAVE ALMOST REACHED McNARN CASTLE. YOU WILL SEE IT FROM THIS BLUFF AHEAD.

I HAVE NOT SEEN IT SINCE I WAS A CHILD.

A MISERABLE CHILD...

I'D FORGOTTEN HOW BEAUTIFUL IT IS...

OF COURSE YOU REMEMBER THE *MACAUAD* CLAN? THEY ARE ALWAYS UP TO SOME *DEVILMENT*, ARE THEY NOT?

WOENER + MORROW 6-10

THEY HAVE CONTINUALLY *ATTACKED* BOTH THE MCNARNS AND THE KILCRAIGS VICIOUSLY, AND WITH *VIOLENCE*.

WHAT HAVE THE MACAUADS TO DO WITH THIS?

I PROPOSE TO YOU THAT OUR TWO CLANS SHOULD SWEAR AN *OATH OF FRIENDSHIP*, AND BAND TOGETHER AGAINST THE MACAUADS, WHO POSE A THREAT TO US AS LONG AS WE REMAIN ENEMIES.

© 1981 United Feature Syndicate, Inc.

WITH MY PROPOSAL, YOUR NEPHEW WILL GO FREE.

IF I REFUSE?

HE WILL BE SEVERELY PUNISHED.

WOENER + MORROW 6-11

BLACKMAIL!

NO. THIS CAN ONLY HELP US BOTH.

© 1981 United Feature Syndicate, Inc.

BUT TO MAKE SURE THAT OUR FOLLOWERS KNOW THAT THE HAND OF FRIENDSHIP WIPES OUT THE BLOOD THAT HAS BEEN SHED BETWEEN US, YOU WILL MARRY MY *DAUGHTER*!

MARRY?!

△107

I AGREE THAT OUR CLANS SHOULD BE UNITED, BUT I HAVE NO INTENTION OF MARRYING!

VERY WELL THEN, YOUR NEPHEW, TORQUIL MCNARN, MUST FACE HIS PUNISHMENT. THE MCNARN NAME WILL BE DRAGGED THROUGH THE DUST.

YOU GIVE ME NO CHOICE,

WHAT IS YOUR ANSWER?

AS CHIEFTAIN OF THE MCNARNS, I WILL MARRY YOUR DAUGHTER AND JOIN OUR TWO CLANS,

SO BE IT,

Having agreed to marry the Kilcraig's daughter, the Duke rides back to his castle in a rage...

BLACKMAILED BY THE KILCRAIGS! I AM A FOOL!

VERY WELL, I WILL MARRY HER. I HAVE NO ALTERNATIVE,

BUT AS SOON AS WE ARE MARRIED I WILL LEAVE HER AND THE CLANS TO THEIR OWN DEVICES AND GO BACK TO ENGLAND. I WILL NOT BE TIED DOWN WITH A WIFE!

The Wedding....

THERE IS THE MAN I AM TO MARRY AND HE WILL *NOT EVEN LOOK* AT ME!

AS SOON AS THIS *RIDICULOUS* CEREMONY IS OVER I WILL LEAVE FOR EDINBURGH. SHE CAN STAY HERE AND *ROT*, FOR ALL I CARE!

With the wedding of Clola Kilcraig and the Chieftain of the McHarns, the two rival clans are joined.....

NOW HE *MUST* LOOK AT ME, I KNOW HE WILL BE *DISAPPOINTED!*

GOOD LORD!!

SO MAY GOD HELP ME AS I SHALL SUPPORT THEE, AS LONG AS MY LIFE LASTS,

SHE'S *BEAUTIFUL!!*

110

SIR, IT HAS BEEN MANY YEARS SINCE I HAVE SEEN YOU. I AM YOUR NEPHEW, TORQUIL MCNARN.

SO *YOU* ARE THE ONE WHO HAS CAUSED ALL THE TROUBLE.

I WISH TO CONVEY MY *APOLOGIES* FOR PLACING YOU IN THE POSITION OF *HAVING* TO MARRY A *KILCRAIG.*

WE WILL DISCUSS YOUR BEHAVIOR **LATER.**

SOMEHOW I AM *NOT AS SORRY AS* I WAS BEFORE.

TO THE *LASTING FRIENDSHIP* OF THE MCNARNS AND THE KILCRAIGS!

HERE, HERE!

YOU SEEM TIRED.

I ... DID NOT SLEEP VERY WELL LAST NIGHT.

NOR DID I.

SOON WE WILL HAVE A CHANCE TO GET TO **KNOW EACH OTHER** BETTER.

I AM CERTAIN WE WILL BE *FRIENDS.*

111

113

WHAT DO YOU MEAN? THE *MACAUADS!*

TORQUIL AND I PLANNED TO CELEBRATE THE ALLIANCE OF THE MCNARNS AND THE KILCRAIGS BY *TEACHING THE MACAUADS A* **LESSON**.

WE WERE GOING TO STEAL A CALF, BUT JUST AS WE WERE ABOUT TO, SOME MEN APPEARED AND *DRAGGED TORQUIL AWAY!*

OH, JAMIE! HOW **COULD** YOU DO ANYTHING SO *STUPID?*

WHERE IS TORQUIL NOW?

THEY ARE KEEPING HIM IN *THE WATCHTOWER* TILL MORNING.

THE *WATCHTOWER!* ON THE MOOR?

YES, UNTIL THEY CAN BRING HIM TO MACAUAD CASTLE TOMORROW. PERHAPS WE COULD *RESCUE* HIM BEFORE THEY COME BACK.

I CLIMBED THE WATCHTOWER ONCE AS A CHILD. *I WILL HELP.* IT WOULD BE *TERRIBLE* IF THE DUKE LEARNED OF THIS!

I'LL SEND FOR SOME HORSES. YOU DO *EXACTLY AS I SAY* AND PERHAPS NO HARM WILL COME OF THIS MATTER.

THE MACAUADS THOUGHT IT WOULD BE SAFE TO LEAVE TORQUIL *ALONE* IN THE WATCHTOWER TILL MORNING. I DID NOT KNOW HOW TO REACH HIM.

I KNOW A WAY.

FOLLOW ME, AND *BE CAREFUL!*

I'M COMING.

ARE YOU *SURE* NONE OF THEM STAYED BEHIND TO GUARD HIM? IT WOULD BE *DREADFUL* IF WE WERE ALL TAKEN PRISONER.

TORQUIL!

CUT HIM LOOSE, JAMIE. *HURRY!*

IT WAS JOLLY SPORTING OF YOU TO RESCUE ME, WE HAD *BAD LUCK,* DID WE NOT, JAMIE?

BAD LUCK! IT WAS *CRASS STUPIDITY!* YOU MUST PROMISE ME NEVER TO DO SUCH A THING AGAIN!

IF YOU *PROMISE* ME THAT, TORQUIL MCNARN, I WILL NOT TELL YOUR UNCLE WHAT *FOOLISHNESS* YOU HAVE BEEN UP TO.

I PROMISE...

115

OH ..., I AM SO STIFF ...

I **MUST** FIND THE DUKE AND TRY TO EXPLAIN TO HIM **WHERE** I WAS LAST NIGHT, I CANNOT LET HIM THINK I WAS MEETING A **MAN**.

WEAVER & MORROW 7/6

THE DUKE'S GONE TO EDINBURGH TO MEET THE **KING**, IF THAT'S WHO YE'RE LOOKIN' FER. I NEVER SEEN A MAN SO ANGRY AS **HE** WAS THIS MORNIN'!

© 1981 United Feature Syndicate, Inc.

HE HAS GONE ALREADY?

YES, HE HAS.

THE DUKE HAS GONE TO EDINBURGH THINKIN' HIS NEW BRIDE IS **UNFAITHFUL** ..., HE WILL NEVER RETURN TO YOU!

WEAVER & MORROW 7-7

© 1981 United Feature Syndicate, Inc.

YE'RE LOOKIN' PALE AND TIRED, I'LL FETCH YE SOMETHIN' TO EASE YER HEAD.

I..., THANK YOU, I AM TIRED.

122

WILL SHE BE ALL RIGHT?

SHE'LL RECOVER. SHE'S CALLIN' FER YER UNCLE, MASTER TORQUIL...

THE DUKE ...*THE DUKE*... I MUST *EXPLAIN*... THE DUKE HAS GONE TO EDINBURGH TO SEE THE **KING** ...TO EDINBURGH...

THE DUKE HAS GONE TO EDINBURGH TO SEE THE KING! OH, TORQUIL! MRS. FORSE ...HER SON ...HER SON EUAN MEANS *TO KILL THE KING!*

I *REMEMBER* NOW! MRS. FORSE TOLD ME HER SON MEANT TO KILL THE KING! YOU MUST TELL THE DUKE ...GO TO EDINBURGH! *WARN HIM!*

LIE BACK NOW, DEARIE.

NO, NO! TORQUIL!

YOU ARE SURE?

YES!

I'LL GO *AT ONCE.* I'LL TAKE TWO MEN WITH ME AND IF IT'S POSSIBLE WE'LL GET THERE *IN TIME.*

HURRY! *HURRY!*

WEAVER + MORROW 7-18

123

In Edinburgh...

I HEAR YOU HAVE *MARRIED* CLOLA KILCRAIG, OLD BOY!

YES ...

WHY DID YOU NOT BRING HER WITH YOU ... ARE YOU *JEALOUS*?

DO *YOU* KNOW MY WIFE?

WEAVER & MORROW 7/20

WHEN SHE LIVED IN EDINBURGH WE WERE ALL *IN LOVE* WITH HER, BUT SHE WOULD HAVE *NONE* OF US!

OH?

IN EDINBURGH? AND SHE WOULD HAVE NONE OF YOU ... PERHAPS I HAVE *MISJUDGED* HER ...

I CANNOT *STOP THINKING* ABOUT HER ...

YOUR GRACE—

YOUR GRACE, THERE IS A YOUNG MAN HERE WHO IS *TERRIBLY ANXIOUS* TO HAVE A WORD WITH YOU.

WEAVER & MORROW 7/21

IS IT NOT TIME FOR THE *KING'S PROCESSION*?

UNCLE! YOU MUST *LISTEN*!

TORQUIL! WHAT IS *WRONG*?!

124

IS THERE ANY WORD FROM THE DUKE?

NONE, YOUR GRACE. TRY TO GET SOME REST, NOW. YOU ARE LOOKING PALE.

I PRAY TORQUIL WAS *IN TIME* ...OH, **WHERE** IS THE DUKE! I MUST TALK TO HIM ... **EXPLAIN** ...

WHAT AM I SAYING? THE DUKE WAS *FORCED* TO MARRY ME, AND NOW HE THINKS I AM *UNFAITHFUL*! I WILL *NEVER SEE HIM* AGAIN!

I AM IN LOVE WITH A MAN WHO DOES *NOT LOVE* ME. I MUST FACE IT BRAVELY—

CLOLA...

YOU!

WAS TORQUIL *IN TIME*?

WE CAUGHT EUAN FORSE JUST AS HE WAS ABOUT TO FIRE AT THE KING. BECAUSE OF *YOU*, THE KING IS SAFE.

The End